A boat chugs near the river bank.

Down the River

Written by Paul Harrison

Collins

Down the river you can see a lock.

long boat

A kingfisher darts down to get a fish.

wings

Rivers join and get bigger.

reeds

soil

rushes

9

In the tunnel it is too dark to see.

11

Bigger boats join the river further down.

tugboat

sailboat

On the river

🐾 Review: After reading 🐾

Use your assessment from hearing the children read to choose any GPCs, words or tricky words that need additional practice.

Read 1: Decoding

- Practise reading words with more than one syllable together. Look at the word **river** on page 2. Say the word and clap each syllable as you do. Ask the children to sound talk and blend the letter sounds in each syllable "chunk": ri/ver.
- Then ask them to blend the sounds together.
- Do the same with the words **tunnel** and **kingfisher**.

Read 2: Prosody

- Choose two double page spreads and model reading with expression to the children.
- Ask the children to have a go at reading the same pages with expression.

Read 3: Comprehension

- For every question ask the children how they know the answer. Ask:
  - Can you remember the name of the river boats we saw near the river bank? (If necessary, look at page 5). (*long boat*)
  - What did the long boats travel through in the pictures? (*a lock, a tunnel*)
  - Can you remember the name of the boats we saw "further down"? (*tugboat, sailboat*)
  - Which type of boat would you most like to go on? Why?
- Discuss why some rivers have locks. (*to help boats go uphill and downhill safely. In the photo on pages 2 and 3, the lock's water level is slowly reducing so the boat can go downhill.*)
- Look at pages 14 and 15 together. Talk about the long boat's journey down the river.